THE WORLD OF MUSIC
Classical Music

Published by Creative Education
P.O. Box 227
Mankato, Minnesota 56002
Creative Education is an imprint of The Creative Company.

DESIGN AND PRODUCTION BY ZENO DESIGN

PHOTOGRAPHS BY Corbis (Archivo Iconografico, S.A.; Austrian Archives; Bettmann; Dennis Marsico), Getty Images (Alfred Eisenstaedt//Time Life Pictures; Rischgitz; Kent Smith; YOSHIKAZU TSUNO/AFP; Alvis Upitis)

Copyright © 2008 Creative Education.
International copyright reserved in all countries.
No part of this book may be reproduced in any form
without written permission from the publisher.
Printed in the United States of America

LIBRARY OF CONGRESS CATALOGING-IN-PUBLICATION DATA

Riggs, Kate.
Classical music / by Kate Riggs.
p. cm. — (World of music)
Includes index.
ISBN 978-1-58341-564-1
1. Music—History and criticism—Juvenile literature. I. Title.

ML3928.R54 2008
781.6'8—dc22   2006102981

First edition

9 8 7 6 5 4 3 2 1

Classical

MUSIC

KATE RIGGS

CREATIVE EDUCATION

Classical music is an old kind of music. It started over 300 years ago. Classical music has lots of rules. People who know all the rules write the music. They write it for other people to sing and play.

Classical Music

Early classical music was written by hand

THE WORLD OF MUSIC

A man named Bach (*BOK*) helped start classical music. He wrote music for lots of instruments. The organ was his favorite instrument. An organ has lots of pipes. The pipes can make many different sounds. Some sounds are low and rumbly. Some sounds are high and squeaky.

Bach loved to play the organ. He wrote almost 250 songs for it.

|| *Classical Music* ||

Bach was very serious about music

Another man named Stradivari (*strad-uh-VAIR-ee*) made great instruments. He made them out of wood and strings. Lots of people liked them. They liked how his violins could sound like people's voices. His violins could sound angry. Or they could sound calm.

Stradivari made lots of cellos (CHEL-ohs). A cello looks like a big violin.

Classical Music

Violins and cellos have four strings

|| THE WORLD OF MUSIC ||

People can play instruments alone. Or they can play in groups. People who like to play in groups play in orchestras (*OR-keh-struhs*).

The person who leads an orchestra is called a conductor.

|| Classical Music ||

The conductor sometimes plays along

Some orchestras are big. Some orchestras are small. Orchestras can make music go fast or slow. They can make music get loud. They can make music get soft.

Classical Music

Orchestras can have many instruments

THE WORLD OF MUSIC

A man named Mozart (*MOAT-zart*) wrote lots of music. He wrote very fast songs. He wrote very slow songs, too. He wrote music for orchestras. He wrote music for singers. He wrote music all the time!

Mozart wrote his first songs when he was only five years old!

|| *Classical Music* ||

Mozart was always writing music

THE WORLD OF MUSIC

A man named Beethoven (*BAY-toe-ven*) wrote good music, too. Some of his music was sad. But some of his music was happy. People liked to listen to all of his music.

Beethoven went deaf. But he kept writing music.

|| *Classical Music* ||

Beethoven could hear music in his head

After Beethoven died, classical music changed. It did not sound like classical music. It was too **modern**. Lots of people did not like it. They wanted classical music to stay the same.

|| *Classical Music* ||

Classical music can be exciting

THE WORLD OF MUSIC

Classical music keeps changing today, too. But lots of people like it. They like to play it. They like to listen to it, too. Classical music is played all over the world!

People can play classical music at almost any age.

Classical Music

Some classical music includes singers

GLOSSARY

deaf when someone cannot hear sounds

instruments things people play to make music

modern different from things in the past

rules things that tell people how to play something

violins instruments made out of wood and strings; the strings help make the sounds

Classical Music

A concert hall, where orchestras play

23

INDEX

Bach 6
Beethoven 16, 18
cellos 8
changes 18, 20
conductors 10
Mozart 14
orchestras 10, 12, 14
organs 6
rules 4
Stradivari 8
violins 8